Overview *Seeds*

Seeds travel in many ways and are found in many places.

Reading Vocabulary Words

dandelion

coconut

tumbleweed

High-Frequency Words

fruits	ground
inside	things
stick	pets
socks	grass

Building Future Vocabulary

* *These vocabulary words do not appear in this text. They are provided to develop related oral vocabulary that first appears in future texts.*

Words:	*jelly*	*food*	*favorite*
Levels:	Purple	Orange	Orange

Comprehension Strategy
Classifying and categorizing information

Fluency Skill
Reading smoothly

Phonics Skill
Consonant digraphs: *th* (<u>th</u>e, <u>th</u>ey, <u>th</u>is, <u>th</u>em, <u>th</u>ese, <u>th</u>en), *ch* (bea<u>ch</u>, pea<u>ch</u>es)

Reading-Writing Connection
Making a list

MW01065174

Home Connection
Send home one of the Flying Colors Take-Home books for children to share with their families.

Differentiated Instruction
Before reading the text, query children to discover their level of understanding of the comprehension strategy — Classifying and categorizing information. As you work together, provide additional support to children who show a beginning mastery of the strategy.

Focus on ELL
- Display seeds from seed packets. Have children look at the shapes and put them in groups according to appearance.

- Have children preview the photographs and tell what they see on each page.

Using This Teaching Version

1. Before Reading

2. During Reading

3. Revisiting the Text

4. Assessment

This Teaching Version will assist you in directing children through the process of reading.

1. **Begin with Before Reading** to familiarize children with the book's content. Select the skills and strategies that meet the needs of your children.

2. **Next, go to During Reading** to help children become familiar with the text, and then to read individually on their own.

3. **Then, go back to Revisiting the Text** and select those specific activities that meet children's needs.

4. Finally, finish with Assessment to confirm children are ready to move forward to the next text.

Building Background

- Write the word *coconut* on the board. Ask children to tell what they know about coconuts. Tell children that all nuts are actually seeds from which new plants can grow.

- Introduce the book by reading the title, talking about the cover photograph, and sharing the overview.

Building Future Vocabulary
Use Interactive Modeling Card: Word Web

- Introduce the word *jelly*. Ask *What kind of jelly do you like on your sandwiches?*

- Write *jelly* in the center of the Word Web. Have children write names of different kinds of *jelly* in the rectangles.

Introduction to Reading Vocabulary

- On blank cards write: *dandelion*, *tumbleweed*, and *coconut*. Read them aloud. Tell children these words will appear in the text of *Seeds*.

- Use each word in a sentence for understanding.

Introduction to Comprehension Strategy

- Tell children they will be using what they know to think about how things in *Seeds* are alike and can be put into groups.
- Look at the photograph on the title page together, and ask children to say how the objects in the picture are alike. (They are all seeds.)

Introduction to Phonics

- Say these words aloud and write them on the board: **the**, **then**. Ask *What beginning sound do you hear?* (/th/) Point out that the letters *th* make this sound. Repeat for **then**.
- Say **peach** and write it on the board. Ask *What sound do you hear at the end?* (/ch/)
- Have children look for other words in the book that begin with *th* and contain the digraph *ch.*

Modeling Fluency

- Read aloud page 2 to model reading smoothly.
- Point out that as you read, you do not stop and hesitate. Read page 2 again, and have children echo you to practice reading smoothly.

2 During Reading

Book Talk

Beginning on page T4, use the During Reading notes on the left-hand side to engage children in a book talk. On page 16, follow with Individual Reading.

During Reading

Book Talk

- **Comprehension Strategy**
  Display the cover of *Seeds.* Say *Describe the dandelion seeds.* (They are small and white and brown.) *Do all seeds look like dandelion seeds?* (no)

- Encourage children to predict what they will learn in *Seeds.*

Turn to page 2 – Book Talk

Seeds

By Heather Hammonds

Seeds

By Heather Hammonds

Future Vocabulary

- Ask *What is this book about?* (seeds) *What seeds are your favorite to eat? Why?*

Now revisit pages 2–3

Book Talk

- **Phonics Skill** Say the word *these*. Ask *What sound do you hear at the beginning of* these? *(/th/) What letters make the sound /th/? (t, h)*

- **Comprehension Strategy** Show the seed packets on page 2. Ask *Which seeds are vegetables?* (beans, squash, snow peas, herbs) *Which is a flower?* (petunia)

- Ask *What do seeds need to grow into plants?* (water, sun, and soil)

Turn to page 4 – Book Talk

New Plants

Look at all of these seeds!

Seeds grow on plants. Then new plants grow from the seeds.

2

Seeds need water.

They need sun and soil, too.

New plants will grow from seeds if they have water, sun, and soil.

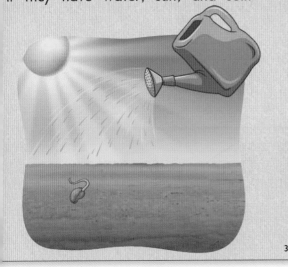

3

Future Vocabulary
- **Comprehension Strategy** Say *Look at the seed packets on page 2. Which seeds will become a food?* (beans, squash, peas, herbs)

Now revisit pages 4–5

During Reading

Book Talk

- Ask *How can the wind blow the dandelion seeds away?* (The dandelion seeds are light; the wind catches the white part like a kite.)

- Have children locate the words *dandelion* and *tumbleweed* on pages 4 and 5.

- **Comprehension Strategy** Ask *How are the tumbleweed and dandelion seeds alike?* (They are both carried to different places by the wind.)

Turn to page 6 – Book Talk

Seeds and the Wind

Some seeds blow away in the wind.

This dandelion has lots of seeds. The wind blows the seeds away. New dandelion plants will grow from the seeds.

4

This tumbleweed rolls around in the wind.
Seeds fall off the tumbleweed as it rolls around.

5

Future Vocabulary

- Say *For some people, looking at nature is one of their favorite things to do. What is your favorite thing to do?*

Now revisit pages 6–7

During Reading

Book Talk

- Have children locate the word *coconut*.

- **Comprehension Strategy** Ask *How are the small seeds on page 7 and coconuts alike?* (They are seeds that fall into the sea. You can find both on the beach.) *How are dandelion seeds and coconuts alike?* (They both travel away from the parent plant.)

- **Phonics Skill** Have children find the word *beach*. Ask *What ending sound do you hear?* (/ch/) *What letters make the sound? (c, h)*

Turn to page 8 — Book Talk

Seeds and the Sea

Some seeds can go a long way over the sea.

Coconuts are seeds.

They fall from coconut trees onto the beach.

The sea takes them to a new beach.

Then new coconut trees will grow.

coconuts

6

coconut trees

seeds

These seeds fall from plants
and can go in the sea, too.
We can find seeds on the beach.

Future Vocabulary

- Ask *What food do you see on pages 6 and 7?* (coconut) *Have you ever tasted coconut? What does it taste like?* (milky, sweet) *What does it look like inside its shell?* (white)

Now revisit pages 8–9

During Reading

Book Talk

- **Phonics Skill** Find *that* on page 8. Ask what sound it begins with and what letters make the sound. (/th/; *t, h*) Have children find more words that begin with *th* and say them aloud. *(then, these, them, things)*

- **Fluency Skill** Read aloud page 8, modeling how to read smoothly sentences of different lengths by taking breaths at appropriate times.

Turn to page 10 — Book Talk

Seeds That Stick

Some seeds stick to things.
These grass seeds
stick to our socks.
We can take the seeds
off our socks and put them
on the ground.
Then new grass will grow.

8

Grass seeds stick to our pets, too.
They are sticking to this dog's paw!

Future Vocabulary

- Say *These seeds are sticky. Can you name a food that is sticky? Jelly is a sticky food. When do we eat jelly?* (in sandwiches, on toast) *Does jelly have seeds?* (It can.)

Now revisit pages 10–11

9

During Reading

Book Talk

- **Comprehension Strategy** Say *The maple tree seeds fly. What other seeds fly in the air?* (dandelion seeds)

- **Phonics Skill** Have children find and read aloud the words that begin with /th/. *(these, that, they, then, the)*

- **Comprehension Strategy** Ask *If you were making a group of seeds that are little, which seeds that you have seen so far would you include?* (dandelion, gum tree, tumbleweed)

Turn to page 12 – Book Talk

Tree Seeds

Little seeds can grow into big trees.

These maple tree seeds have wings. The wings help the seeds to go a long way from the tree. Then new maple trees will grow.

10

These gum tree seeds are so little
that they are hard to see,
but they will grow
into very big trees.

gum tree seeds

11

Future Vocabulary

- Say *Think about all the seeds you have read about so far. Which seed is your favorite? Why?*

Now revisit pages 12–13

During Reading

Book Talk

- **Comprehension Strategy**
  Ask *How are the seeds in berries alike?* (They are small; we eat them; they are good for us.) *Which berries are red?* (raspberries, cranberries, strawberries)

- **Fluency Skill** Read page 12 to children. Model how to read smoothly without hesitation.

Turn to page 14 – Book Talk

Seeds and Fruit

Some seeds grow inside fruit.

Berries are fruit.
There are lots of little seeds inside these blackberries.
Birds eat the blackberries.
They take the seeds to new places.
Then new blackberry plants will grow.

12

blackberrie

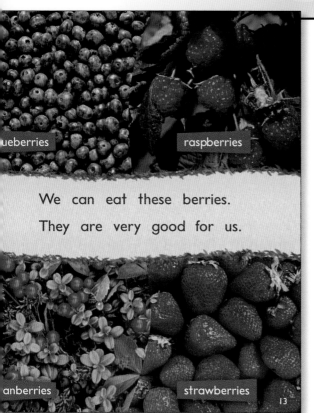

ueberries

raspberries

We can eat these berries.

They are very good for us.

anberries

strawberries

13

Future Vocabulary

- **Comprehension Strategy** Ask *Which of these fruits would you use to make a good jelly?*

Now revisit pages 14–15

During Reading

Book Talk

- **Comprehension Strategy** Ask *How are the seeds on pages 12–15 alike?* (They are all fruit seeds.) *Which fruits have big seeds?* (plums, peaches)

- **Phonics Skill** Have children find a word on page 15 that has /ch/. *(peaches)*

Turn to page 16 – Book Talk

Big seeds grow inside the plums on this tree.
Birds like to eat the plums, but they do not eat the plum seeds.

New plum trees will grow from the seeds.

14

plums

14

anges

apple

These fruits have seeds inside them, too.

erries

peaches

15

Future Vocabulary

- **Comprehension Strategy** Say *All of the fruits on these pages are used as food. Which of the foods are mostly red?* (apple, cherries, peaches) *Which are blue?* (plums) *Which foods are so big that you can only fit one in your hand?* (oranges, apples, peaches, plums) *Which foods can you grab by the bunch?* (cherries)

Go to page T5 – Revisiting the Text

15

During Reading

Book Talk

- Leave this page for children to discover on their own when they read the book individually.

Individual Reading

Have each child read the entire book at his or her own pace while remaining in the group.

Go to page T5 –
Revisiting the Text

Seeds We Eat

We can eat some vegetable seeds.
We eat pea seeds and bean seeds.
We eat corn seeds, too.
The seeds are very good for us.

Can you think of some more seeds we eat?

peas

corn

16

During independent work time, children can read the online book at:
www.rigbyflyingcolors.com

Revisiting the Text

Future Vocabulary

- Use the notes on the right-hand pages to develop oral vocabulary that goes beyond the text. These vocabulary words first appear in future texts. These words are: *jelly*, *food*, and *favorite*.

  Turn back to page 1

Reading Vocabulary Review
Activity Sheet: Word Wheel

- Have children write *coconut* in the center of the Word Wheel.

- Have children write words that describe a coconut in the top half of the wheel and words that do not in the lower half.

Comprehension Strategy Review
Use Interactive Modeling Card: Making Conclusions

- Write these conclusions on the left side of the card: *1. Many seeds travel far away from their plant. 2. Fruits are good for us to eat.*

- Have children find sentences in *Seeds* to support the conclusions. Have children make their own conclusions and support them.

Phonics Review

- Have children take turns looking for words in the book that begin with *th* or contain /ch/.

- Have children work with a group and brainstorm other words beginning with *th* or containing /ch/. Have them use four of the words in a sentence.

Fluency Review

- Partner children to take turns reading page 16. Remind children to read the sentences before reading aloud to make sure they know the words.

- Monitor each reader to see that he or she reads smoothly without stopping to decode or recognize words.

Reading-Writing Connection
Activity Sheet: Summarizing

To assist children with linking reading and writing:

- Model summarizing information for children.

- Have children complete the Summarizing chart for *Seeds.* Then have children compile and illustrate a list of their favorite seeds.

Assessing Future Vocabulary

Work with each child individually. Ask questions that elicit each child's understanding of the Future Vocabulary words. Note each child's responses:

- What is your favorite fruit to eat?
- What foods grow in a garden?
- When you do like to eat jelly?

Assessing Comprehension Strategy

Work with each child individually. Note each child's understanding of how to classify and categorize things he or she has read about in the text:

- Which seeds are good to eat? Which are not?
- Which seeds are carried away by water?
- Which seeds are round and flat?
- How are the seeds in raspberries, strawberries, blueberries, blackberries, and cranberries alike?
- How are the seeds in plums, cherries, peaches, oranges, and apples alike?

Assessing Phonics

Work with each child individually. Provide magnetic letters for each child to create words with *th* and *ch*. Note each child's responses for understanding *th* and *ch* digraphs:

- Did each child recognize words that begin with the letters *th*?
- Did each child recognize and properly pronounce *ch* in the middle or end of a word?

Assessing Fluency

Have each child read page 14 to you. Note each child's understanding of reading smoothly:

- Did each child look over the sentences before reading to make sure he or she knew all the words?
- Did each child pause at appropriate places, such as at the end of sentences?

Interactive Modeling Cards

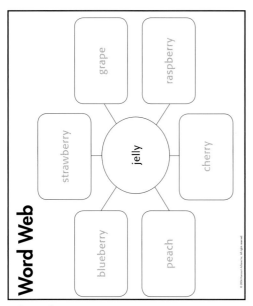

Word Web

grape
raspberry
strawberry
jelly
cherry
blueberry
peach

Directions: With children, fill in the Word Web using the word *jelly*.

Making Conclusions

Conclusion	Details from the Book
Many seeds travel far away from their plant.	Some seeds can go a long way over the sea.
Fruits are good for us to eat.	We can eat these berries. They are very good for us.

Directions: With children, fill in the Making Conclusions chart for *Seeds.*

Discussion Questions

- What kinds of seeds do people like to eat? (Literal)
- Why do you think it helps seeds to travel on clothes, in the wind, and in a pet's fur? (Critical Thinking)
- What fruits and vegetables have seeds that we don't eat? (Inferential)

Activity Sheets

Word Wheel

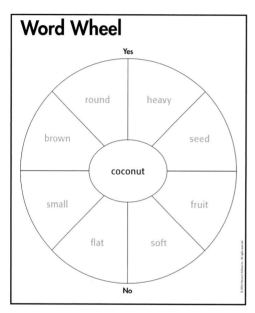

Yes

round | heavy

brown | seed

coconut

small | fruit

flat | soft

No

Directions: Have children fill in the Word Wheel using the word *coconut*.

Summarizing

Page	Summary
2–3	Seeds grow on plants. Seeds need water, sun, and soil.
4–5	The wind blows seeds around.
6–7	The sea carries seeds to new places.
8–9	Seeds can stick to things.
10–11	Big trees can grow from little seeds.
12–13	Berries are seeds we can eat.
14–15	Other fruits have seeds inside, too.
16	We can eat vegetable seeds.

Directions: Partner children and have them complete the Summarizing chart for *Seeds.*

Optional: On a separate sheet of paper, have children compile and illustrate a list of their favorite seeds.